POEMS

by

DUNSTAN THOMPSON

1943

SIMON AND SCHUSTER, NEW YORK

MANUFACTURED IN THE UNITED STATES OF AMERICA
BY THE VAIL-BALLOU PRESS, INC., BINGHAMTON, N. Y.

To

John Felker

ACKNOWLEDGMENTS

Some of the poems in this volume have appeared in *The New Republic, The Harvard Advocate, Vice Versa, Furioso,* and *New Poems: 1943.* The author thanks these publications for permission to reprint.

CONTENTS

WATER MUSIC

Over the river, sleeping, sleep your nights
Of never my delights, of famous flights,
Not mine, outshining moonstone stars, displayed
Like summer sailors from black water drawn
To dance on malachite, to prance parade
Past queens last-quarter afternoons of dawn,
First sunset mornings, break-of-day midnights,
O as the snow swans end their Rhenish flights.

Over the river, sleeping, sleep your dreams,
Where heir apparent or presumptive seems
Already king to Nibelung, gold dwarf,
Mock maiden, and the jewel box knave at hearts,
Each standing on the beach, each on the wharf
To wave farewell to you, whose birdboat starts
Rising from submarine savannahed dreams,
O as the mermaid is the merman seems.

Over the river, sleeping, sleep your love,
Ice as the crystal moon, so soon the dice
Of death, announcing lunar empire here,
Fall like the songs of lorelei, like all
The bishop's towers, like flowers, like every tear,
While you, child of the mist, at last, must call
Green knight from water grave to dive for love,
O as my eyes are seven on your dice.

MEMORARE

Remember, at this moment, O somewhere
The plane falls through the indifferent air,
No longer flying the about to be dying
Pilot to any over-the-border disaster, but lying
Like the boyhood toy, by bad luck destroyed.
   The lost lads are gone
   God grace them

Remember how, even now, when the ship sinks,
The sailor, paler than a pearl, only thinks,
Diving through destiny to be invested with coral,
Of himself—saved from the sea caves where no laurel
Lives—and so gives up a gay ghost at land's end.
   The lost lads are gone
   God grace them

Remember, also, as the soldier in amber fires
Too late, his nerves, swerving on exploded tires,
Plunge through the past to exhaust their history
In the silent, never again to be violent mystery,
Which the womb worshiped more than the hero's tomb.
   The lost lads are gone
   God grace them

Remember—do not forget—the numbered, anonymous spy's
Suddenly surprised, not quite clever enough disguise,
And see him, neither gallant nor grim, obeying
The code, sans cipher, of the classroom saying:
O happy and hallowed to die for a flag.
  The lost lads are gone
  God grace them

Remember the enemy, always remembering you,
Whose heartbreaks heartbeat defeats, who too,
Shedding tears during prayers for the dead, discovers
Himself forever alone, the last of his lovers
Laid low for love, and, O at your mercy, murdered.
  The lost lads are gone
  God grace them

HYD, ABSOLON,
THY GILTE TRESSES CLERE

Your eyes like islands lure the wanderer now
From salt-sea travels, water world of tears;
And welcome, O as hyacinthine spring
After a wintertime, your lips allow
Expense for roses on a lawn of spears
To show the soldier who is killer king.

What wisdom has the heart which worships God
Only by indirection, by grace of gold
And tiger hair, extravagant like sun
Light? How is praise made perfect when the nod
Of a halcyon head exalts my hand to hold,
Heraldic acolyte, this sword-shaped gun?

The question never finds an answer: boys
Who take to talking take to drink as well;
And I, rejected now by heroes, write
My name like mist around the secret convoys
Of those I love, whose dogwatch kept, still tell
Glass beads for one another through the night.

You too are one of them. You also mean
The figure from the frieze, the scarlet page
At stirrup, groundfall, mercy in between;
So I must martyr you, must disengage
My heart, that sad spectator, from a scene
Where war unwinds you like a clock—but my age,
O myrmidon of doom, shall see you seventeen.

THIS LONELINESS FOR YOU
IS LIKE THE WOUND

This loneliness for you is like the wound
That keeps the soldier patient in his bed,
Smiling to soothe the general on his round
Of visits to the somehow not yet dead;
Who, after he has pinned a cross above
The bullet-bearing heart, when told that this
Is one who held the hill, bends down to give
Folly a diffident embarrassed kiss.
But once that medaled moment passes, O,
Disaster, charging on the fever chart,
Wins the last battle, takes the heights, and he
Succumbs before his reinforcements start.
Yet now, when death is not a metaphor,
Who dares to say that love is like the war?

DREAMS OF
THE BARRACKS EMPEROR

My summer season like a winter weather
Comes cold as reason to love's faithful heart,
And where were once the sun and moon together
Eclipsed with stars, now voids of vanity impart
Their lonely, O by clock crow, space of time.

My noonday zenith makes meridian laughter
Turn tears at midnight— Look, the pumpkin plane!
Not torches then to light this flier after
His bombardiers of glass: but falling rain
Puts out the flares for pilots, lands him in the dark.

What vision of violence can I plead for pardon?
I walked the streets, a stage star hearing cheers
From blackout boys, whose lucent cats' eyes—in the garden
Later at leave-taking—ran me through like shears.
Guards! Guards! Blood on the white rose, death by thorns.

TARQUIN

The red-haired robber in the ravished bed
Is doomsday driven, and averts his head,
Turning to spurn the spoiled subjected body,
That, lately lying altar for his ardor,
Uncandled, scandalizes him, afraid he
Has lost his lifetime in a moment's murder:
He is the sinner who is saint instead;
This dark night makes him wish that he were dead.

What daring could not do, the drinks have done:
The limbo lad communicated one
Last sacrament, and, fast as falling, heaven
No longer held a stranger to emotion,
Who, like a star, unsexed, unshamed, unshriven,
Was hurled, a lost world, whirling past damnation:
Circled by chaos but by eros spun,
The devil burned much brighter than the sun.

This bellboy beauty, this flamingo groom,
Who left his nickname soul too little room
For blood on blades of grass, must now turn over,
Feel for the fatal flower, the hothouse sterile
Rose, raised in no god's praise, and, like death, never
Again enjoyed, must make his madness moral:
Washed by the inland waters of the womb,
The salt sheet is his shroud, the bed his tomb.

THE POINT OF NO RETURN

See him now, how unhurried he destroys
The tick-tock meaning of the nursery boy's
Nostalgia for love's never-never land,
And, fairy-story prince turned toad, spews out
Not pearls, but girls' garters, when wizard wand
Waves him unwanton, just a Times Square tout:
His smile mints money, but his laugh enjoys
The spoilt child buying back pawn-broken toys.

This all-day sucker for a one-night stand
Gambles his good luck on a steady hand
With queer cards, odd dice, zero numbers, all
Falling by fate too late to lose him health,
Wealth, happiness—gold bricks that build a wall
Around pride's pleasure park with much less stealth
Than rats use, abusing his heart—unmanned
By mother memories more than rats had planned.

Lo, victor, he is vanquished by a small
Miscalculation in a barroom brawl,
Goes for the gutter, makes his getaway
Through sewers, cesspools, urinals, and slums,
Back to the tenement where he can play
His passion to the blandishment of bums:
There, decked with heroin, he has his hall
Of mirrors where no cops can ever call.

What welter of the womb that air breath day
The serpent signified once more in clay:
Later, the data of a Christ-crossed class,
The garbage gift of faith, slag heap of hope,
Concerning charity—the sounding brass:
Those cardinals triple crowned this antipope,
Whose keys are skeleton, whose ring is gay
With fools for jewels, whose blessings playboys pray.

His life—thus, your life, my life—his life has
Its double-feature legends, myths of jazz,
O, Raffles on the roof, O, moon in June,
So, like a blackjack hero, he upsets
The blind queen's balance at the game—but soon,
Too soon, and lovelost by a tune, forgets
His jukebox record plays when X-Men pass:
"The head is human but the eyes are glass."

VILLANELLE I

For George Barker

The train is disappearing down the track
Bound for the border which the gunmen guard:
It is not likely that you will come back.

More easy to defend than to attack
Your verses show the errors you discard:
The train is disappearing down the track.

You are so young the genius that you lack
Is time which makes the diamond point so hard:
It is not likely that you will come back.

The clever critic and the charming claque
Are just the justice your high court disbarred:
The train is disappearing down the track.

Your comet light flashed bright when night was black
And showed how holy heaven could be starred:
It is not likely that you will come back.

These are the cinders from the engine stack
That float across the vacant railway yard:
The train is disappearing down the track.
It is not likely that you will come back.

VILLANELLE II

For John Gesner

The dark is danger though it dawns each day.
Disaster knows me as a mother does.
The sun will set no matter what I say.

This paradise, or pleasure park, is gay
At noontime only. Night destroys the rose.
The dark is danger though it dawns each day.

Sirens are silent; panpipes cannot play;
Their melodies are mute; their songs dumb-shows.
The sun will set no matter what I say.

The faun must leave the forest, go away
To summer countries where Narcissus grows.
The dark is danger though it dawns each day.

So spring presents the garden god. This May
His murder is more marked than men suppose.
The sun will set no matter what I say.

The boatman takes my penny for his pay.
Disaster knows me as a mother does.
The dark is danger though it dawns each day.
The sun will set no matter what I say.

DEATHSCAPE WITH MEGALITHS

Living but never loving, you, whose star shines
Ice age of loneliness for friends, implore
The watcher by the clock, but marvelous signs
Like zeros indicate the dial is set for war.

Oh, I could tell your time, if time to tell
Struck once, or twice, not three strokes ever. But
My hands are bloody, red-nailed, bound to ring
Alarms, excursions, cries without. Where the bell
Hangs, I hang too. No soldier with sword can cut
Me down, the hangman hung, whose death-day song I sing.

All tunes are changed by chance, all colors fade
As fast as dyes can run, and all wise words
Are witless when the writing stops. Have I obeyed
Commands, or only followed free? Like sea birds
Circling a shipwreck, fears fly down; nightmares
Swoop round me; doubts are deadset, plunge from the start.
What I would say I cannot say. But in your prayers
Remember me, if not, O my camoufleur, in your heart.

SONG

Waiting for the telephone to ring,
Looking for a letter in the box,
Daydream minion, he is nightmare king,
Timeless lover who has stopped the clocks.

Time revolts: he abdicates as king,
Lives his exile in a land of clocks,
Waiting for the telephone to ring,
Looking for a letter in the box.

THE END IN VIEW

Not always to beware the outstretched hand,
The friendly word, the loving look. And never
Forever to discover the arctic strand,
The winter kingdom where the snowman excites
No season of summer, where the northern lights
Are only auroral to the iceberg's endeavor;
The place of frozen water, the cold land.

Somehow to understand each other. To see
That the mirror image is a piece of glass;
The bullet, meant for everyone but me,
I shoot myself; the elegy, a celebration
Of gladness, not sadness. Let the hero pass,
Facilis descensus, the avenue of tombs,
His pride death daunts, his pomp the dust dooms;
All columns fallen, the arch gone down. But we
Are not heroes so long as the heart is strong
To praise God's grace in the one beautiful face,
Whose gaze, gold against the sun, an exaltation
Of indifference is. So let us like angels trace
High heaven with stars to make a morning song,
And let us, O Loving, move the mountains from their base.

JACK OF HEARTS

I

Loving you more than myself, I offer only
The mirror broken, O at the first word spoken
By you: quicksilver argent through all marrow
Of skull and skeleton; Christ's crystal token,
Spun from the showcase—the one place where the lonely
Hero, passing the glass, reflecting his sorrow,
Looks for the devil, and is rarely mistaken:
Behold the jewel for any fool to borrow.

But I am no thief. For this my grief is formal,
A manner, so to speak, of giving pleasure
To you, who measure me, but not with metric
Standards, nor assay my worth by faith in normal
Laws of balance. You cause the keeper of the treasure
To diamond-cut the bloodstone from the rhetoric.

II

There was no bell. Nor telegram to tell
Me: "All is lost. Flee for your life." Nor call
Intoned by the telephone: "Be warned in time.
For there's no coming back, no second chance."
Nor fancy glance beckoning me aside to rhyme
"Beware" with "There." Nor hand that appalled the wall,
Writing, writing, writing: "There was no bell."

Time is, time was, time's yet to be. Love grants
The absolution of the dove to temporal crime,
Breaks the mirror, stops the clock, and in the fall
Brings back the spring to every wishing well.
So in that moment, moment of no time at all,
What zenith bell you rang, what crisis chime
Pitched high, O ever higher than my angel chants.

III

Exaggeration of sensation shows
The poet loves a person not a poem.
So you, my dangerous darling, my delight
And doom, are like the tomb tricks Merlin knows;
The foolish fever, holidaying schoolboys home;
And, O so once again, the plane in flight.

All poems are praise, all lust a kind of love.
But I celebrate the fate of those whose diffidence
Led them instead of passion; who were of
That passive nation featuring the future tense;
The what have we here, better the half a loaf;
All looking-glass lads who found their class a defense
Against not being a bastard; those always above
The in-want-of-a-word battle. For them I write you nonsense.

IV

Here where there is nothing to fear except life,
I find the knife in the wound, the blood-red blade
Arrayed against my so-called heart. And all the art
Of witchcraft, such as I laughed at once, is prayed
For now. How if those killer sisters, crazy to start
Operations of love, thrice be bitch, each be my wife.

My destiny is hastened, O not by a star but a war,
And somewhere, yes, already, I march out to disaster,
Not needing to guess the place by blessing a better
One for you. But what does it matter whom it is for,
So long as the fact is death. Meanwhile, and much faster,
While my hands drop from the clock, your airmail letter
Canonizes tomorrow, and, though yet to be written, means more
To me than poetry, means not the furies at the door.

CIRCULAR TERROR

After the drink, and after much too much
To think about—the bills; unanswered letters
From friends now fathom fived by war, who touch
Like nerves a wound; and envy of my betters
For poems I cannot write—after all this,
I am persuaded by a second drink
To try another bitch betrayal, kiss
Good-by my swimmer when he starts to sink.

My debtors sand the seven seas, suggest
Eternity like any Jesuit Joyce
Of words. My money and my mercy wrest
Away from me the foghorn's haunted voice
That praises rock of ages. I am lost,
Lilac and lavender, a faded south
Of sweetheart roses, pink as a drink, that cost
Only a wordless gesture from my mouth.

The land of desolation rises out
Of water dreams where looms my drunken boat,
Cargoed with love apples, red as ruin, rout,
Rebellion—end of friendly Jacob's coat,
Too many colors. I protest my wit
Is shipwrecked by the lack of sailor's art
To read my compass. Drink disasters it,
And with it breaks once more the cut-glass heart.

LARGO

For William Abrahams

Of those whom I have known, the few and fatal friends,
All were ambiguous, deceitful, not to trust:
But like attracts its like, no doubt; and mirrors must
Be faithful to the image that they see. Light bends
 Only the spectrum in the glass:
 Prime colors are the ones which pass
 The less distorted. Friendship ends
In hatred or in love, ambivalence of lust:
Either, like Hamlet, haunted, doting on the least
Reflection of remorse; or else, like Richard, lost
 In vanity. The frozen hands
 That hold the mirror make demands;
And flexing fingers clutch the vision in a vise.
Each one betrays himself: the ghostly glazer understands
  Why he must work in ice.

All friends are false but you are true: the paradox
Is perfect tense in present time, whose parallel
Extends to meeting point; where, more than friends, we fell
Together on the other side of love; where clocks
 And mirrors were reversed to show
 Ourselves as only we could know;
 Where all the doors had secret locks

With double keys; and where the sliding panel, well
Concealed, gave us our exit through the palace wall.
There we have come and gone: twin kings, who roam at will
   Behind the court, behind the backs
   Of consort queens, behind the racks
On which their favorites lie who told them what to do.
For every cupid with a garland round the throne still lacks
    The look I give to you.

The goddess who presided at our birth was first
Of those in fancy clothes fate made us hate to fight:
The Greeks with gifts, good looks, so clever, so polite,
Like lovers quick to charm, disarming, too well versed
   In violence to wear weapons while
   They take a city for a smile.
   By doomed ancestral voices cursed
To wander from the womb, their claws plucked out our sight,
Who nighttime thinking we are followed down the street
By blind men like ourselves, turn round again, and wait,
   Only to hear the steps go past
   Us standing lonely there, at last
Aware how we have failed; are now the Trojan fool
For all the arty Hellenistic tarts in plaster cast:
    The ones who always rule.

We are alone with every sailor lost at sea
Whose drowning is repeated day by day. The sound

Of bells from buoys mourning sunken ships rings round
Us, warning away the launch that journeys you and me
  On last Cytherean trips in spring.
  There the rocks are where sirens sing
  Like nightingales of death. But we,
Hearing excitements, music for the ear, have bound
Our voyage to find its ending where the sterile sand
Spends pearls and coral on a skull. The sailing wind
  Is with us now and then: blows high
  As halcyon clouds across the sky:
Falls fast to doldrums while the moon is also young,
Untided, half to harvest whole. See how our sirens die
    Before their song is sung.

What we have always wanted, never had, the ease,
The fame of athletes, such happy heroes at a game,
Beloved by every likely lad, is not the same
As what we have: these measured methods how to please
  An indolent and doubtful boy,
  Who plays at darts, breaks for a toy
  The sometime valued heart. Why seize
The moment in the garden, on the stair, to blame
Our nameless Eros for his daring? Too little time
Is left for love. When we come back, what welcome home
  Will he award our wounded eyes?
  What uniform be his disguise
In dreams, when sleeping sentries always march away

— 23 —

Once more to war? Now is our novelty: we may surprise
   The faun at end of day.

Make no mistake, my soldier. Listen: bugle calls
Revoke your leisure like a leave, invade your peace
With orders on the run, and, loud as bombs, police
Your life for death. The poet's blood-brick tower falls:
   Even his vanity is gone,
   Which leaves the loser all alone.
   Not private poems, but public brawls
Demand his drumbeat history, the pulse that must increase
Until his heart is ransomed from its jewel. Revise
Your verse. Consider what king's killer did to those
   Who wrote their way between the shells
   That last delusive time. Farewells
Are folly to our serpent queen. She will not sign
Discharge of conscience for a masterpiece, but, hissing, tells
   Failure in every line.

We are the mountaineers who perish on the slopes
Of heaven high and perfect Himalayan peak:
Exhausted by the cold, we can no longer speak
To one another—only signal by the ropes.
   Those best before us have, alas,
   Plunged through a gentian-blue crevasse:
   The snow-blind flaw. Their glacial hopes
Shine as a stream of desperate stars, icebound, and bleak,

That mock their nimbused glory from a frigid lake.
Where we stand now, they stood much farther: climbing like
   Legendary guides. But traps
   Were waiting for their last collapse:
Inviting visions from the moon world air—misplace
A step to follow, dance to death. They fell, so we, perhaps,
   May do as well with grace.

Now noble guests depart for good, wearing our loss
Like flowers. O Damon, decked with asphodel, who moves
Among the shadow dwellers. But he shall hear the hooves
Of unicorns at gallop, see them, coursing, toss
   Their fluted horns above the cool
   Unpoisoned waters in love's pool,
   And, kneeling, lay their heads across
A beatific virgin's breast. The day approves
His passage: sunlight on the secret river gives
Bright benediction to his boat. Elysian waves
   Bear him, the hero, far from us
   To join the gods. Illustrious!
No words may worship him. The laurel is not all
That withers at the roots, since we, lamenting him, are thus
   Autumnal for his fall.

Armed, say you? Armed, my lord. So, likewise, you and I,
Who with the butchered ghost must stalk the battlements,
Shall watch—cold-comfort guards—how lonely lie the tents

Where strangers sleep together just before they die.
    Look where their banners in the air
    Are half-staff hung. The cockcrow dare
    Of dawn is mourning in the sky.
Our thoughts like bayonets blood time. What precedents
Of passion shall we use to brave the coward? Once
Bombs are as roses, will he kiss the black-heart prince?
    Honor, more heavy than the sea,
    May overwhelm both you and me
To give no quarter choice at all: gay boys, whom war
Won janizary; youths, who flung away their shields. So we
    Are *mort à Singapore.*

Narcissus, doubled in the melting mirror, smiles
To see himself outfaced by tears, and, sorrowing, hands
His ace of love to harlequin of hearts, who stands
The distant edge of laughter. Time's joker still compiles
    Trick score of triumph, trumps the queen
    To play his knave of emeralds. Green
    Gamester reflects the water guiles
Of palming, reads the gambled cards, and then demands
Another pack to shuffle. But the glass partner bends
The fate five fingers round a saint's stigmata, wounds
    By dealing diamonds from his nails.
    No marveled metaphor avails
To vantage this beloved impersonator twin,
Whose coronet, crown crystal, qualifies a peer. My voice fails.
    In your name poems begin.

LEAVE PRIDE TO THOSE
WHO HAVE ALREADY DIED

Leave pride to those who have already died.
Even in heaven they need it more than you;
There—where no one is lonely, where by your side
Stands the lover of ever you—there the two
Completely one celebrate the state of the sun,
Famous at last, past peril from hell's cold harm,
And, O time rhymed, beginning, not yet begun,
By angels gloried, circle the center of their charm.
But now only humility is the right disguise,
For the devil, good-looking as a movie star,
Moves among us, conversing his clever lies
Over music and drinks and pleasure, at war
With what we want most though it cost our art,
The end of every poem, the always loving heart.

ARTICLES OF WAR

I

The dead young man stood up in his grave:
"Grieve, grieve for me," he said. "I was brave
As the best of you successful few
Who followed your hero home from war,
Haloed with laurel leaves that grew
Like legends and curled like snakes your hair.
I was there—but not to live, not to save
Even the life-given love I gave.

O wave, wave to me across the loss
Of laughter, and, after you pass, toss
Me what are more than flowers in your smile;
While I, death's dandy, string these tears
For pearls on unstrung years that while
Away no daytime fame like yours.
The mask of memory greengrows the moss:
But where the worms work—there is my source.

You, false to me then, be true instead
Now when the stone crown crushes my head,
Be the king's friends when no king reigns
Save in the exiled grave, be the bell
That rings from hell my famous thanes,
Be court, be kingdom, be my most of all,
Be mindful of me in the loveless bed."
The dead young man went back to the dead.

Fell forward in the west, as far as forward fell,
Red star, the blood star, O zodiac of death's farewell:
   Like lucklost plane spun also all
   My heart: like parachute was peace
     To flower a foolish wish
For you, who over airways ever call
To landing field of love where no planes crash,
    Where the bombs cease:
I wished your star of war no time of crime to tell.

When your ship sailed, O Almirante, my Marvel of Peru,
South through archipelagoes of grief I followed you,
   Where snakes like pearls coiled undersea
   Equators round drowned albatross
     Of loss—leviathan
As loneliness was Amazon to me:
The viceroy boys, meridian in green,
    Saw my Atlantics cross
Themselves for your imperial Pacific view.

Hunter who haunts the dawn consorting unicorn
Was echo tally-ho to sally forth when faun
   Returned like triumph to the fern
   And forest pool of fall: was gay
     As gala ghost in spring:

Took up the chase with grace, looked out to earn
That tapestry of scene where queens lie long
    In dalliance for a day:
You held him happy, heard halloo of hunting horn.

And, O as music then, you were like dancing, psalm
King entrancing, slingshot shepherd boy, whose calm
   Of tears was smiles to overwhelm
   The face of longing, who with a kiss
     Trapped no elaborate lures
For swift or starling, but, my darling, an elm
Tree tower to bower the birds of paradise:
    What words I had were yours
When love's regalia, orb, and scepter crowned your palm.

Not the Hawaiian horror, no, nor the scream of doom
Time radioed, when air raid struck each college room,
   Put Johnny on the spot: his name,
   Already listed like the lost
    Pale sailors with their ships,
Leads off those elegiac dead who claim
Tomorrow for their sorrow, who laugh at last
    No longer then, whose lips
With kisses should, my wonder, O be flowers to bloom
    Before the unknown lover's tomb.

III

The boy who brought me beauty brought me death;
Like laughter he came after me, came through
The dew of danger to come down to earth.

Not as I dreamed he seemed, but as a stranger
Met at a railway rendezvous—a new
Announcer on the deadly nightshade hour.

But strong as anger and powered from every finger,
Skyhigh his hand commanded me to flower
My dragon tower with love's heroic rose.

Who throws the flame, corona crests his name
Like lilac Lucifer? who flaring goes,
Galaxy of glitter, hailing stars in hell?

I could tell as well the tiger to be tame
As ask this prince of risk how now he fell:
His secret is more brazen than a bell.

My ace of swords is words away from doom;
And I am made a merry maypole groom:
A jack of hearts, life's fumbling tumbling fool.

All my immediates are here: the fear
Of failure follows Narcissus from the pool
Cool as a death's-head to his bed of glass.

Alas, the leaves are red that feed on blood,
Are torn by thorns to valentine the grass:
My garden grows when winter snows are near.

But now is not for fancy dancing doubts
When war shouts down dead aeroplanes, down flood
Of fliers flapping wings like eagle scouts.

This is the kiss of peace, my dove of death,
To weave like laurel through your olive wreath:
Now strike the hour and let time's towers break the earth.

IV

Whirled in the waltz when by the bagpipe skirled,
Our fun was done with laughter, went after tears
And terror—war's era, like a searchlight curled
With night around the sound of planes, appears
   O as love above the falling years.

Not you nor I are drawn by dawn, who sight
The bright before the morning moon of sorrow:
West, while the dragons over Asia fight,
East, as the swans of Europe die, we borrow
   Time whose clocks and mirrors mock tomorrow.

Revolvers fire their salvos: poems like a kiss,
The instant whisper pledging peace, outrage
Not the heart already, but the mouth to miss
The pulse of peril when the lips engage:
   Death is the chance we take to come of age.

Whether alone with loneliness, or gay
At drinks in the cabaret of fallen angels,
Our doom is easy through the room: there to stay,
Lazy, voluptuous, waiting—equate the angles,
   Springs like the lion and like the leopard mangles.

Our season of success has every minute hands
To gesture haste—no words to waste, and shows,
A finger on the danger, where our stranger stands

Ready to rifle us of luck: the devil knows
   How many marvels we could still propose.

But if the specter on the stair is there
At all, the sunlight on his hair shall cherish
Green crowns of flowers: though powerless queens despair
Of honor, gold is the mold for kings who perish
   Like Lucifer with hell for passion's parish.

So we are lost, by careless history filed
As smiles and memories for the famous friend:
Still we, chancing romantics, must be heiled
With Hitler by the human omens of our end:
   Even our souls forgiven, ourselves pretend.

Suppose you had by heart the stressed heroic lines,
To act the part—elected, had Hamlet's choices,
Would you choose well? and I—say fame defines
My poems with those whose seraphim rejoices,
   Would I be graced with such celestial voices?

No: we are children wastreled by the war,
Idle mollycoddles, mothers' darlings, fools
Who fancy aunts to air their summer seashore:
In short, the lads who love their lovely schools:
   Murder is horror: like love breaks all the rules.

There's little left, and what is left is leaving
As fast as trains we missed, or beauties kissed:
Check cashed, and, canceled, bill: no use deceiving
Ourselves that we are final on death's general list.
   Like time is nothing more for me to tell:
   Yet, at this moment, O I wish you well.

V

At the end, at the end, there is time,
Like the past, like the past, to be mourned
Over and over again, but the time
Is so short, is so short, I am warned
O to spend with a friend my last time.

So with life I would have you be gay
As the carnival waltz at a dance,
All glitter, all lights, always gay
Like laughter, champagne, a romance
With the one who has fun being gay.

May the talk, may the joke, may the kiss
Still stay for a day, for a week,
While the smile on the face that you kiss
Stays still as a place, when you speak
Not a word to be heard but a kiss.

At the end, at the end, there is love
To mock time in the mirror, the clock,
Which I turn back, returning like love
Is returned by the tide to the rock,
O to send to a friend my last love.

ORPHIC SONG

Midnight is time enough to call
Eurydice to life. Alas
For poets then, when crystal all
Walls of glass bend, if Orpheus pass
Along the corridors of hell.

She tells her devil he is bright
Light of laughter; is outlaw
To only heaven's purblind sight:
Who might, love's hero, singsong more
Than angels out of Charon's boat.

But he, goat, peacock, pretty boy
Of bells and wishing wells, cannot
Be flattered. He, the satyr, annoy
Him as she may, will clock the dot
Of twelve, alive like moon by day.

Away from him, she sees her life
Ascending passageways of death,
Turn as a burnt-out flame, a knife
Interned to stop her yearning breath
For false spring, April showered by grief.

Half harlot, half Elysian queen,
Whose lover praises no one when
He looks too soon, unseen
Eurydice must mother men
Like sunset sons who see no sign.

WHERE IS THE CLOCK
TO TELL MY TIME OF TEARS

Where is the clock to tell my time of tears,
That strikes like midnight when love's hands are noon?
Or where, while diastolic tide of fears
Flows over me, find out the utter ice-floe moon?

Now I am serviced by a pageboy smile
As doors revolve me through a lounge of brass.
Who passed for millionaire across the pile,
So soft my mirror broke into a snow of glass.

Happy I was but happy shall not be,
Outfaced by luck as fancy as a tart.
Nor may I go to bed today and see
Tomorrow less like sorrow break the heart;
Since what was more exciting than a football game,
No longer watched with love, is not for me the same.

GLISTERING PHAËTON

For George Barker

The light was lava to explode your heart
When crowns of fire were kingly to your head:
The mountains of the moon gave up their dead.

The countries of Atlantis saw you start
Ascending through dimensions of the sea:
The dolphins drew your chariot to me.

As stars were seven, so the sun was one
To aureole your landfall in the west:
For you the swans were singing at their best.

A pride of lions was triumph to the gun
Fauns fired when unicorns unfurled your flag:
The local peacocks had no cause to brag.

Here you have seen the loveless river run
In cut-glass torrent to the bay of saints:
The pool of pity that Narcissus paints.

You have explored the ruined city where
Time takes no time to do his jungle duty:
The serpent-twined and bat-infested beauty.

Plateaus of peace you found whose desert air
Loomed like an avalanche to catch the breath:
The last mirage before the pass of death.

You drew a map of praise with drops of blood
Raising a poem to name each place of rest:
The phoenix asked you to remain his guest.

When you had gone the Pole began to flood
The Gulf Stream with the melted ice of love:
The current changed to let the ocean move.

The silent winter spoke of you in flowers
To bring the birds of paradise to spring:
The bells of morning heard their welcome ring.

As land of gold proclaimed in fanfare hours
So orient your passing brought it birth:
The continent now novel to the earth.

May gods be gracious to the favorite one
Dynastic in succession to the sun:
O may your day be only just begun.

PRINCE ATLANTIS

For Sanford Shanley

Shall we play sudden death or vantage games?
Be instant heroes, be the Alexander boys
From Babylon to Baghdad, from seven Troys
To seventy-seven the cities sexed with sterile names
Of phoenix; false flamingo; peacock; parakeet;
Coiled coral snake—cruel by the brackish water tank;
Love leopard; eunuch monkey; blind lizard—blank,
Twice zero-eyed before the sun. Where always heat
Lies lascive on the terrace, hanging garden, court
Of eastern embassy—despite the melons, ice
In sherbets, frigid wine. Where afternoons of dice
Move midnight; while the chessmate king and queen consort
Together over pawns in gambit. Where you and I,
Alone, and lost forever in the desert, die.

Across time's cricket field your bright pavilion stands
For schoolboy games—the tragic past observed with tea.
Where love applauding saw the lover score his century,
Who, rifled now, and bowled by bombs, not friends, commands
The silent common room. Where lazing, laughing came,
Bravo in blazer, gay, good looks for all, the Lochinvar
Of lads, initialed in so many desks, whose only war
Was wonderful for sudden winning—dead like his name,
Memorial on nothing more than notes in study hall,

Or stranger's face too quickly seen. Where no one knew
The sporting pilot in the prefect so remotely kind to you;
For none construed *O lente, lente* meaning not at all
"Run slowly, slowly, O horses of the night," but like you tried,
Faustus, to turn back time: so many have already died.

Astronomer Royal! Look! Sky-gaze my astrologic star,
Ascendant Virgo in the House of Mars: turn telescope
To circuit satellites, rock moons, revolvers mocking hope,
Whose adamantine mirrors, made murderous like holy war,
Whirl without ending. O my meteor worlds—fire sans desire,
Volcanic glass. But you, the greenman, Prince Atlantis, chart
Ocean where tides are turbulent; by every planetary heart
Drawn—danger to caravel of love; where always islands tire
Horizons, once more exhausted, once more miraged with clouds.
Since not by seeming safe does dolphin save the sailor, drowned,
He fears like always, under surf of words: and whether crowned
Or not with seaweed, amorous Neptune, trident in the shrouds
Of every Grecian ship, sinks captain for the sake of crew:
Yet you, Leander still for swimming, think your Hero true.

THANE OF GHOSTS

While lights flash double meanings, dot and dash
Their cipher message, code whose key is love,
My mathematic dazzle dives like crash
Landing plane, where pilot spins, perilous of
Self-satisfaction, through no triple point
Approved to airdrome happy slant of wings:
But, rebel rather, whom not smiles anoint
With benediction, I, as elsewhere kings
Wore courage more than crown, return my plane
Like Newton's apple down to death again.

Once more, once more, and still once more, I raise
Outrageous banners on my kingdom come
Of continents, O isthmus where all ways
Atlantic spend themselves Pacific, home
Ten thousand leagues from home, and dearer, yes,
Than boyhood bays where paper galleons rode
To anchor, mother marveled, first success
At make-believe of life: but now, bestowed
Like luck to almost suicide, my new-found
And wonder world extends love's golden ground.

Cabala, crystal, ouija board, and pack
Of queens, where every ace is death, foretell
Time's thriller-diller danger, night attack

On welcome worshiped to a fare-thee-well,
Whose house of cards, doom castle quite in Spain
Dissolves, dead-level, when esquire of looks
Loving leaves, for what disaster, green demesne:
Then neither letters serve for patent, books
For herald heart at arms, but, sweet my lord,
Tomfool is joker, Jack whose tricks are scored.

All thoughts are thieves that plunder me of you,
Lay waste love's landscape like a winter, make
Meantime midnight, Macbeth of dreams, review,
Deadmarch, my Duncans, bloody heads that shake
So grizzled locks, and point the dagger out
That did them in, when neither tears nor prayers
Cried: "Hold! A graveclothes masquerade shall rout
You from stone throne of state, and double dares
Of death shall come by dawn." O, Banquo, see,
Your boy from Birnam Wood now murders me.

OCEANIC ODE

Braided like bravo, gold as gay day gallant,
Love's ensign flagged my fleet, decked ship with signals,
O more than commodore, commanded cannon
Fire forever.

You were so many snapshot minutes, such perfect
Photographs of fun. Time's black-page album
Displays you for a picture-postcard witness:
This charmed the traveler.

I see you now, the fancy boy of heroes,
Bold as if life were ballet, you the dancer,
Who—swan surrounded by romantic robots—
O'er leap the future.

But history hates the humble, pins her ribbons
On flagrant butterflies whose wings mean murder;
So you, exalted not from radio station,
Like poems are precious.

Where gardens once, where fountains always flowering
Kept summer solstice through the rose of autumn,
Now leaves are canceled. Triton springs from water
Fall to winter.

So see war's salamander burn, fire angel;
Emblazed with swords like fencer foil the dragon.
Even the submarine success is doubtful:
How drowns the German?

Surrender not. There are no sweet surrenders
Left to the lonely, left to those whose longing
For friends explodes a lifetime charge. I wish you
Fair winds, my sailor.

IMAGES OF DISASTER

For Alfred Green

I

Who salvaged not my deep sea dredged my shallows:
O fished me out like suicides, like anchors—
Blood rust on both: then threw me back, all-hallows
Dumbstruck. From Venice carnival to Greek-fire tankers

By plane I came, so quick, so sudden shifted:
Not wax-winged Icarus, drowned, what water-welter
Sunset of salt, what tear-crowned pearls. But lifted
High, higher still, and highest, saw the dead-time delta

Outblack Africa, flood tide for war. Marked, flashing
Island to island, fly, like hundred million,
The murdering Minotaurs—*in excelsis*—crashing
Perpetual spires, rubble and ruin, no green Avilion

Of life left. Beheld, gazer, thus dove violenced,
Sand castle, postcard-pretty park, the fountain palace,
And my fair lady, London Bridge—all silenced.
Not sleeplight in garden, ghostly father, grail chalice

Crossing above the rose tree, thorn tree, rood tree
Made me a vision. Starset I looked: unfolding
Their Flanders poppies, cannons rose, and showed me,
In sex of seconds, Venusberg of death. But holding

My heart under glass, still in my hands, from Dover
Was wafted East, and, over swanland, marveled
At mouse-plagued river: regarded the vultures hover
Like luck above the loon king's lake—by no bombs rivaled.

Mazurka, polka, polonaise: music, deceitful
As mirrors, whirled my memory, waltz for wonder,
Through sound of shells, machine-gun fire. Fateful,
This feather-floating angel heard, not thunder

Baroque, rococo, but fall, like summer season,
Dead white, the wedding-cake disastered city.
North Northeast, Northeast by North: there treason
Of weather glazed my glance, froze polar pity

Blue ice of sorrow. But eagle still, imperial
Assassin, witness watched, when flag-flown color
Of blood was banner, waved for snowman's burial
Beside the bullet's harvest hero. What killer

With kisses then could matter me, death's darling,
And gay boy of ghosts, whose eyes, sapphire no longer,
Gored, dazzle dagger, God's good-looks. Now the starling
Fast flew me home: O nothing said, no word of anger.

II

Nautilus, deciding at an early age that he
Was different from the others, my merman wore
Mother of pearl, his mistress jewel, life's undersea
Surviving lonely light. From siren sweet-sung shore

Absent as time, he plunged, boy bold, not moonbeam
So cold, but colder, down, glass meteor of ice,
To doom. Plunged. More silent there than any daydream,
His water wonder without shadow wandered, where voice

Ding-dong, aerial, weeping rang no buoy bell so deep.
But further fathom dived than whale, dove Davy Jones
His locker loose, where, Lo! the emerald dead, asleep
Lay languid. Those whose beautiful and oceanic bones,

Less opulent than only coral, treasure trove
Him madman, wave wracked, moving among enameled wrecks
Like Perseus, pirate prince of ships, who, rocked by love,
Unchained his captive's nacreous, O salt-sewn, novel sex.

Through cobalt caves, stalagmite columned, groined
Androgyne—translucent washed, the traveler breasted waves,
Quartz crystal swimming. Sand-shifted Naiads never joined
Largess of arms so amorous: who, keeping kelp-grown graves,

Shrouded by shells, said Nay, said Nay, for no one, no,
Would they unwind their glowworm hair. Grottoes of green
Gold glittered his eyes; while levitator serpents, slow
As bubbles, blew up, warm weather, father fortune. Obscene

The Old Man of the Sea, octopus, his paramour, kissed
Not once such heirloom lavished luck, but, stranglehold,
Embraced, all feelers fierce, his lovely lad. Mirror mist
Around him, Neptune-drowned Narcissus, lax limbed, rolled

Fancy free: then fled him far. Cross currents swirled
Him past Sargasso longitude of longing—where no tide
Turns turbulent: no surf. Whirled monsoon mad, and curled
Like combers, came he dolphin through the foam. There glide

And glisten of scales played him, pretty porpoise sport,
Aquatic gambols, fun with fish. Sudden as Fundy Race,
More sudden so, he saw the submarine by depth bomb brought
To grief. Like flotsam floating, the death-deflowered face

Of a sailor sorrowed him: and once, not for himself, he wept.
But hurled high heaven, holocaust of oil, his geyser speed
Fired him to fleet the singeing sun: O, matchless, not accept
The giddy god from flying Greek machine. Fell down gay Ganymede.

III

"Preclude, preclude," he said, "love's first and lasting judgment.
Not every flier comes to kill. This mask of stranger
Dominoes no bully boy from gallows tree. Engagement
Fought at airdrome, mooring mast, or landing stage puts danger

Beyond the range of romance—fly high, fly low, dying
Is still the same sick falling out of guts. Grave gravitator,
Tumbler for tombs, black ace to spades on bedrock lying,
Lord Lancelot of Larks is dead. The faun as instigator

For lilac elegies—such as you say you write—may fancy
Himself, unarrowed, forever jewel and silver marrowed,
Triple rhyming God's mainspring timing. Who knows? His chancy
Bravado beats pulse of saints, who, more than heroes, harrowed

Like setting Son the root-red soil of hell. My friending
Of fauns was schooltime life for lovers. Now novel and luckless
Boys, whose every violence probes the bomber's nerve-rack ending
With pierce of pity to the bowels, falter. I see them, reckless

As fashion in the hats for pretty girls, go queer, go glamour
Eyed, go wild as Jesus Christ across His holy horror heaven
To wound themselves with wonder. Gelded catamites clamor
For heart rubies, diamond-tortured clubs, but pilots seven

Dice devil's score by crashing ivory bone to splinters
Of what their worships call the soul. We wear no gold-fleece collars.
The snow moon, murderous, the ice star, shot with bloody winters,
Signal our searchlights: no more easy money. O the green dollars

Of gay days we shall never spend again! I think our sadness
Is such we drop more tears than bombs, more tenderness than terror.
The enemy mans our controls. But bridgeheads of this madness
Are held for minutes: the bombardier corrects his error.

Love like the lancer shatters us. However lively
May that lady be, however quick this lad for laughter,
So soon as either would lie down from dancing, gravely
The gentleman in death's-head uniform, who follows after

Torches and tinkling music, draws back the spider curtain
From bride bed, boy bed, death bed always, to offer only
The kiss and knife-thrust both at once. Now nothing is certain
But being far from home. Survive me for a friend: lonely

As you may be, I shall be lonelier—by the sea invested
With green waters, or by the cruel earth to time be broken.
Remember. Legions will come, the lionhearts, the laurel-crested,
Who demand a requiem. Speak for us them," he said. "I have spoken."

IV

Now every meeting means a new farewell:
With armies levied by the loss of friends.
Sailor and airman each go off. Who shall tell
The last one left good-by again? Childhood ends

For the toy soldier: bugles, drums, the moated fort,
All come alive: war's monstrous magic lantern shows
Gigantic grown the man of lead. How short, so short
The springtime was, the charming river walks with those

Whose every gesture was a gay one, whose words
Rippled like rapids, flashed, spun, sparkled, and ran
In waves of laughter through the college. Season of birds
And violets in the courtyard. Evenings that had no plan

But turned to triumphs: music from the phonograph—
Waltzes, the German jazz: and always too much gin to drink.
Or those long late drives to pleasure parks: the happy half
An hour on the carrousel: a chocolate horse whose eyes were pink.

And there were other nights, in the blue room, so all alone,
Reading Marvel, the perfect poet, with world enough and time
To twist conceits for one, who, though he read, was never done
In asking why the moon was cheese. What lost romantic rhyme

Scheme, tangled like treason, wound metric masquers in a maze
Of heartbreak? Still there was fun—so much, and once or twice
The game was worth, O, all the candles that have burned in praise
Of beauties melted down to wax. Another light: but the price

Is never paid. Illustrious this now historic past
Hangs like a tapestry at which the moths already eat.
For the swagger lad, swashbuckled as a hero, came at last
To join the party. Time's trifler, watching ghost boy beg a seat

Across the table, played foppish with his dilly-dally pen.
He signed the check, looked up, looked up. Disastrous eyes,
Wanton as wounds, gaped with God's terrible tears. It was then
I knew my nighttime had come down. Death and the Devil's surprise

Whirl through the world in search of more to devour. Foretold,
Foretold, I was foretold, how boys shall nothing be by shells,
Shadow like ambuscades the madman's quarry, or cold, as cold
As cowards, ferret for their savaged sex. What victory bells

Are left to ring shall ting-a-ling for these. So let us pray
Grace for the gallants when they stand in love's most need:
And for ourselves, if killer, or if killed, courage to say
Something in prayer for mercy on the friend who is not dead.

ABOUT THE AUTHOR

Dunstan Thompson was born in New London, Connecticut, in 1918. He was educated in England and France, and later at the Canterbury School and Harvard. During one summer abroad, while at Rye, he was a student of Conrad Aiken. At this time, his poetry and criticism did much to enliven *The Harvard Monthly*, which he edited with distinction. He has since published verse in *The New Republic* and *Poetry*. On its spasmodic appearances, his own magazine, *Vice Versa*, was perhaps the most discussed publication of its kind in the United States. Now twenty-five and the youngest poet to be represented in Oscar Williams' anthology, *New Poems: 1943*, he is serving with the Army overseas.